# Bees

by **Judith Jango-Cohen**

**Marshall Cavendish**
Benchmark
New York

Thanks to Mary Perrotta Rich, editor, for skillfully putting it all together.

*For Chris Panetta—a honey of a nephew*

Series consultant:
James C. Doherty
General Curator, Bronx Zoo, New York

Marshall Cavendish Benchmark
99 White Plains Road
Tarrytown, New York 10591-9001
www.marshallcavendish.us

Library of Congress Cataloging-in-Publication Data
Jango-Cohen, Judith.
Bees / by Judith Jango-Cohen.
p. cm.—(Animals, animals)
Summary: "Describes the physical characteristics, behavior, and habitat of bees"—Provided by publisher.
Includes bibliographical references and index.
ISBN-13: 978-0-7614-2235-8
ISBN-10: 0-7614-2235-8
1. Bees—Juvenile literature. I. Title. II. Series.
QL565.2.J36 2006
595.79'9—dc22  2005025610

Photo research by Joan Meisel

Cover Photo: Hans Pfletschinger/Peter Arnold, Inc.

The photographs in this book are used by permission and through the courtesy of: *Alamy:* 27, Wildchromes;
*Corbis:* 1, Anthony Bannister/Gallo Images; 20, Jay Dickman; 40, Scott T. Smith; *Eliot Cohen:* 36, 39;
*Peter Arnold, Inc.:* 4, 8, Ed Reschke; 6, Luiz C. Marigo; 7, 10, 11, 12, 14, 17, 25, 28, 31, 32, 34, Hans Pfletschinger;
9, Jean-Jacques Etienne; 16, Martha Cooper; 18, James L. Amos; 33, C. Allan Morgan;
*Photo Researchers, Inc.:* 22, Valerie Giles; 35, Rod Planck.

Editor: Mary Perrotta Rich
Editorial Director: Michelle Bisson
Art Director: Anahid Hamparian
Series Designer: Adam Mietlowski

Printed in Malaysia

1 3 5 6 4 2

# Contents

# 1 Introducing Bees

Sunbeams melt through the clouds as the last drops of a summer shower spatter the grass. From the warm, wet earth, bees appear. Plump bumblebees drift from their nest—an old mouse house in a moss-covered hole. The bees float in midair for a moment. Then they flit to a field of rose-colored clover.

Bees live on every continent of the world except icy Antarctica. They live in humid rain forests, feeding on a wealth of blossoms. But they also live in dry deserts, searching out the flowers of cactus and other desert plants. Bees even survive on mountaintops where tiny flowers grow in flat mats, snuggled low to the ground to escape frigid winds.

*A bumblebee's fuzzy coat helps keep it warm in cool weather.*

*Butterfly wings are covered with thousands of tiny scales and hairs.*

Scientists have identified more than twenty thousand *species*, or kinds, of bees. About four thousand species live in the United States. Most species are solitary, meaning that each bee lives alone, finds its own food, and builds its own nest. Solitary bees include miner bees, which dig tunnel nests, and mason bees, which mold nests out of mud. Social bees live with other bees in large nests called colonies.

*Like honeybees, ants live in organized groups called colonies.*

Honeybees and bumblebees are social species, as are stingless bees. Stingless bees protect their colonies by biting, not by stinging.

The twenty thousand bee species belong to the group of animals called *insects*. This group also includes butterflies, ladybugs, grasshoppers, and

*A grasshopper can leap about twenty times the length of its body.*

*Ladybugs are beetles, which have hard outer wings.*

ants. Like all insects, a bee begins life as an egg. Then it develops into an adult in a step-by-step process called *metamorphosis*. When a bee hatches from its egg it is a white, wormlike larva with no eyes, antennae, wings, or legs. The larva eats often and grows

*Bumblebee eggs are the shape of rice grains and about half the size.*

quickly. When it is finished growing, the larva spits out a liquid from a silk *gland* below its mouth. The liquid dries quickly into a tough body covering called a cocoon. Encased in its cocoon, the larva becomes a pupa. Breaking free of the cocoon, the white pupa darkens in color and develops body parts, such as legs and antennae. Gradually the pupa changes into an adult.

*The energy from food a larva eats helps the pupa change into an adult bumblebee.*

Like all insects, an adult bee has three body sections. The head contains the mouth, eyes, and antennae. The midsection, called the *thorax*, includes two pairs of wings and six jointed legs. Muscles in the thorax move the legs and wings. The rear section of the bee is called the abdomen. In the abdomen are the heart, the digestive organs, and the *reproductive* organs.

A bee senses its world by seeing, hearing, smelling, feeling, and tasting. Three tiny eyes on its forehead detect light. Two main eyes are located on the sides of its head. The antennae are multipurpose organs. They are covered with fine hairs for feeling and pores for hearing, smelling, and tasting. Bees can also taste with their front feet and with their mouths. Using their senses, bees are able to detect danger, communicate with one another, and go about the business of finding food.

**Did You Know . . .**
A six-day-old honeybee larva weighs 1,500 times more than it did as an egg. If newborn humans grew this fast, a six-day-old infant would weigh about 10,000 pounds (4,535.9 kilograms).

# Feeding from Flowers

With whirring wings, a honeybee darts toward a dandelion and lands on its golden top. It wades into the center, through a thicket of feathery threads. *Pollen* brushes off the blossom and clings to the fuzzy bee's body. Soon the pollen-powdered bee lifts off, looking like a flying flower. Bees use the stiff hairs on their legs to comb off and collect the pollen grains. Pollen is a food that provides bees with protein and vitamins. These nutrients are especially needed by growing larvae and egg-laying females.

Social bees gather pollen for their whole colony, so they pack it into hollows on their back legs. These hollows, rimmed with curved bristles, form "baskets"

*This worker honeybee knows just where to find a flower's nectar.*

to hold the pollen. Some bees pat the pollen into loaves by wetting it with saliva and *nectar*. Nectar is a sweet liquid that bees collect from flowers.

Sugary nectar supplies energy for busy bees. They suck it from deep inside the flowers with their long tongues. A honey sac in front of a bee's stomach holds

*Honeycomb cells are tilted up a bit so the honey doesn't drip out.*

*Honeybees from different parts of the world "speak" different dance languages.*

*A nest is dark, so bees listen to the dance with their antennae.*

18

the nectar the bee harvests. If the bee is hungry, a valve opens, letting nectar flow into its stomach to be digested. Social bees carry nectar home in the honey sac to make into honey.

Bees turn nectar into honey so the honey can be stored as a food supply. Honey does not spoil like nectar. It is higher in sugar and less watery than nectar, so germs cannot live in it. Bees thicken nectar into honey by drying it in the air on their long, tubelike mouths. Honeybees place nectar into wax *honeycombs*. For several days they fan the nectar with their wings to *evaporate* its excess water.

When social bees find a good supply of nectar or pollen, they tell others in the colony about it. Honeybees "dance" to direct nest mates to food. If the flowers are close by, they do a round dance. First they circle one way and then the other. They also give nest mates a sample of the nectar or pollen that they bring back. Using the scent of this sample, the other bees go out and search the area.

If the food is far away, honeybees tell how far it is. They do this with the waggle dance. Buzzing its wings and wagging its abdomen, the bee follows a straight line. Then it makes a half circle, retraces the line

*Most stingless bees nest in hollow trunks or tree branches.*

path, and makes another half circle in the opposite direction. The bee repeats this dance cycle many times. The closer the food, the faster each dance cycle is completed.

The honeybee also lets nest mates know exactly where the food is. If the bee faces upward during the line section of the dance, the food is toward the sun. Facing downward means that the food is away from the sun. Dancing at an angle to the right or to the left directs bees to either side of the sun.

Organizing the gathering and storage of food ensures that the colony will survive. The bees will be able to feed themselves, as well as all the young bees growing back in the nest.

**Did You Know . . .**

Some stingless bee species lead their nest mates to flowers by laying a scent trail. As the bee flies to the food source, it lands on leaves, branches, and stones. At each post it deposits a tiny droplet of scented liquid from glands in its jaws.

# Designing a Nest

A frenzied mass of male miner bees buzzes about on the ground. Several burrow into the dirt and disappear. Soon they emerge from an underground nest with a female clamped in their jaws. She is a newly hatched adult and was digging out of the nest. The males swarm around the female, attempting to mate with her. When one succeeds, the others whir away.

After mating, the female miner bee darts off. From time to time, she hovers over the ground, inspecting the soil. Eventually she selects a spot and begins scraping out an underground nest. When the tunnel is complete, she flies away. The female miner bee returns many times, full of nectar and laden with

*Miner bees are among the first bees to come out in the spring.*

pollen. She places this nutritious mixture into the nest. Then she lays an egg, seals the opening, and leaves. The larva that hatches will find a feast.

Solitary bee species build all sorts of nests. Carpenter bees gnaw out tunnels in woody stems and stalks. Some mason bees make a paste of mud and saliva, packed with pebbles. They shape it into tiny towers. Other solitary bees lay their eggs in empty snail shells. They hide the shell with a tepee of pine needles.

Bumblebee females begin nesting alone, like the solitary bees. They select a nest site under leaves or in an old mouse or chipmunk hole. Then they make balls of pollen and lay their eggs on top of them. To protect the eggs, the bumblebee makes a wax case. She produces the *beeswax* from glands in her abdomen. She chews the wax until it is soft enough to mold. Then she covers the pollen ball and eggs with the wax. Unlike a solitary bee, the bumblebee stays and clings to her egg-filled cases. She warms them by flexing her wing muscles to produce heat. Next to her she keeps a beeswax pot filled with honey. This food supply allows her to eat without leaving the nest.

*Bumblebees sometimes nest aboveground in woodpiles, sheds, or attics.*

All the bumblebee eggs that hatch are females. But these females do not fly off, mate, and lay their own eggs. They stay and help their mother, called the *queen*. These female *workers* gather food and build egg cases and honeypots. Eventually, this frees the queen to concentrate on egg laying.

In the fall, the routine changes. Female workers begin laying eggs. But since these bees have not mated, their eggs are not *fertilized*. These unfertilized eggs will hatch as males, or *drones*. In the fall, female workers also begin feeding extra food to a few of the queen's eggs. These fortified females will become next year's queens.

The future queens mate with the drones and then hibernate over the winter. In winter the workers, drones, and old queen bumblebees die. In spring the hibernating young queens will come out and start a new colony.

Honeybees, like bumblebees, are social. But they have a head start in the spring because their colonies live through the winter. In cold weather, they huddle together in the nest, shivering their wing muscles to stay warm. With the flowers gone, the bees live on large

*A honeybee colony may have up to fifty thousand workers.*

supplies of honey. They store this honey in grids of
honeycomb made of six-sided wax cells. The honeycomb also holds pollen and the eggs the queen lays.
When spring comes, a colony of about fifty thousand
honeybees is all ready to get to work.

# 4 Working Together

A huge hornet heads toward a moldy tree stump. It hopes to seize a honeybee from the nest inside to feed to its hungry larvae. When the hornet lands on the rim of the rotting stump, it is tackled by alert guard bees. Swarming around the gigantic hornet, the bees sting it, paralyze it, and fling it to the ground.

Inside the honeybee nest, business goes on as usual. New worker bees are hatching from the honeycomb. They have been growing and developing inside the wax cell for twenty-one days, since they were laid as eggs. After they pull themselves out, they turn around and clean the cell. The queen will be able to lay another egg inside it now.

*Bees must make new honeycomb when they run out of storage space.*

For the next three weeks the worker will perform different jobs inside the nest. After cleaning for a few days, she will become a nurse bee. Glands in her head will begin to produce liquids called bee milk. She will feed this protein-packed food to the growing larvae for their first three days. Then she will give them bee bread, a mixture of pollen and honey. When wax glands in her abdomen develop she will become a builder bee, making honeycomb. She will also fan the stored nectar to make honey. Toward the end of the three weeks she will take her turn as a guard bee.

The last three weeks of her life, the worker will take on the exhausting job of a field bee. Each day she will fly for miles collecting pollen and nectar. Carrying her weight's worth of food, she will return to the nest. Sometimes she will dance to let other field bees know where to go to find the food.

Another task of worker bees is caring for the queen. During the peak of the summer season, the queen bee lays more than a thousand eggs per day. She does not even rest to eat, so workers take turns feeding and cleaning her. As they lick the queen, they pick up a liquid that she

releases from glands in her head. This fluid is called
*queen substance*. Bees attending the queen pass it on to
field bees when they share the nectar they deliver.
Queen substance quickly gets spread throughout the
colony.

Bees are always aware of the amount of queen substance in the nest. This is because the queen is so
important to the colony. If the queen dies, the bees will

*This honeybee's pollen basket looks full.*

notice the missing queen substance within fifteen to thirty minutes. Worker bees may then start to lay eggs. But these unfertilized eggs will hatch only drones, which do no work in the nest. Only a mated honeybee queen can lay both drone and worker eggs. If the colony is to survive, it will need another queen.

To raise another queen, workers simply break open the cell of a newly hatched larva. They enlarge the cell with wax to make a "queen cell." A queen needs more room to grow because she is bigger than a worker or a drone. Then, instead of feeding the larva bee bread after three days, workers continue to give it enriched bee milk. Several of these cells are prepared. After sixteen days, young queens emerge from their waxen cradles.

The first queen to emerge buzzes about the honeycomb in search of other queen cells. Gnawing openings into the sides of these cells, she stings and kills the

*Three banded Italian honeybees surround their large queen.*

*A new queen honeybee pokes her head out of her extra-large cell.*

queens inside. If another queen escapes from her cell before she is stung, a deadly fight follows. Wrestling each other, each queen bends her abdomen, trying to sting her rival. Although there may be about fifty thousand workers to a colony, and a few hundred drones, there can be only one queen. The victorious queen, just days later, flies into the sky to mate with drones from the surrounding area. Then she quickly returns to the hive to become the colony's new mother.

Eventually, a successful colony with full food stores becomes overcrowded. As a result, queen substance may be spread thin. When this happens, the worker bees will immediately begin creating queen cells, just

34

as though the queen had died. When the first young queen is about to hatch she makes a piping noise. This trumpeting sound is a signal to the old queen. When she hears it, she leaves, or *swarms*, with about half of the worker bees to start another colony. The young queen remains with the rest of the colony. In a good honey year, the swarming cycle may be repeated in a few weeks.

Since ancient times, people have watched these swarms bursting from the nest and swirling into the sky. To ancient people, a swarm was a hopeful symbol. It was a sign of new life.

**Did You Know . . .**

Being a field bee is hazardous work. Crab spiders lurk in flowers. When a bee lands, the spider pierces it with its fangs and sucks out its insides. Some birds nab bees out of the air. One scientist found nearly four hundred dead bees in the stomach of a swift. Skunks, toads, dragonflies, and lizards also feast on bees.

*This crab spider has snagged a bee for a snack.*

# Bees and People

Thousand of years ago, people viewed bees as magical creatures. Some people believed bees were human souls, possibly because they observed swarms of bees whirling up to the heavens. Ancient Greeks believed that bees cared for Zeus, their most powerful god. When Zeus was a baby, bees made honey for him. Out of gratitude, Zeus gave the honeybees their stingers.

People also viewed bees as special creatures because of their ability to make honey. Ancient honey hunters clambered up trees and steep cliffs in search of this sweet substance. It was a marvelous prize in the days before manufactured sugar was available.

*Beekeepers raise bees in hives so they do not have to hunt for honey.*

Finding a nest was difficult though. Sometimes people lured a bee into a box smeared with honey. Then they would try to follow the bee to its nest.

Eventually people learned how to build *hives* to attract swarms in search of a nest. The first beekeepers made hives out of clay pots, hollowed-out logs, and straw baskets. Today beekeepers make hives out of wooden boxes stacked like drawers. Inside each box are rows of frames hanging from ledges. Resident bees build honeycomb on both sides of these removable frames.

Since ancient times, honey was known to have many special properties. Because germs, such as some bacteria, cannot live in honey, it was used as a medicine to heal infections. Honey was considered to be such a perfect food that it was offered at shrines to the gods. It was also known to be a healthy food for people. A three-thousand-year-old Hindu book says, "Let one take honey . . . to beautify one's appearance, develop one's brain, and strengthen one's body."

Today we know that bees provide more than just honey. Many plants need bees to fertilize them so they can make seeds. How do

*A swarm of bees gathers outside its new home in a hollow pipe.*

bees do this? Pollen clinging to a bee's feathery hairs brushes onto the flowers it visits. Pollen is made by the male part of a flower. It must reach the female part of a flower for a seed to develop. Although some plants have both male and female parts, many cannot *pollinate* themselves. They need insect help to move pollen from one plant to another to make seeds. These plants and bees rely on each other to exist.

*Flowers feed bees, and bees keep flowers blooming.*

Although ancient people did not know about pollination, they somehow understood the importance of bees. The Egyptians linked bees with the life-giving sun and rain. They believed that bees arose from raindrops made by the sun god, Ra. Their religious writings tell us that when Ra sheds tears upon the warm, wet earth the bees appear.

Our world would be quite different if there were no bees. Bees of many species pollinate about seventy-one of the world's one hundred major food crops. If it weren't for bees we would not have apples, almonds, carrots, cucumbers, oranges, onions, tomatoes, and tea. So whenever you enjoy a slice of juicy watermelon or carve out a Halloween pumpkin, thank a bee.

**Did You Know . . .**

If you wear light-colored clothing you are less apt to be stung by bees. But perfume and scented hair sprays or lotions may attract bees. If a bee comes near, you should slowly cover your face with your arms, then stay still or slowly back away. Sudden movements or swatting at a bee may alarm it and cause it to sting. If a bee enters your car, pull off the road and open the windows so the bee can escape.

# Glossary

**beeswax:** Yellow to grayish brown wax secreted by the honeybee to construct honeycombs.

**drones:** Male bees, which hatch from unfertilized eggs. Male honeybee drones are bigger than workers but smaller than queens.

**evaporate:** Change from a liquid into a gas.

**fertilize:** The joining of male and female reproductive cells.

**glands:** Organs that release substances that help the body to function.

**hive:** A container built to house a colony of bees.

**honeycomb:** Six-sided wax cells built by honeybees to store honey, pollen, and developing bees.

**insect:** An animal with three body sections, six jointed legs, and no backbone.

**metamorphosis:** Changes in an insect's body structure as it develops from egg to adult.

**nectar:** The sugary liquid made by flowers to attract insects. Social bees turn nectar into honey.

**pollen:** Protein-rich reproductive cells produced by the male part of a flower.

**pollinate:** Transferring pollen from the male parts of flowers to the female parts of flowers.

**queen:** Often the only reproductive female bee in a colony.

**queen substance:** A substance produced by glands in a queen bee's jaws that is passed to all members of the colony.

**reproductive:** Producing others of its kind.

**species:** A particular type of living thing.

**swarms:** Worker bees leaving the nest with a queen to start a new colony.

**thorax:** The middle section of an insect's body of which the wings and legs are a part.

**workers:** Female bees that work inside the nest and collect food for the colony.

# Find Out More

Books

Allman, Toney. *Killer Bees*. Farmington Hills, MI: KidHaven Press, 2004.

Claybourne, Anna. *Bees and Wasps*. Mankato, MN: Stargazer Books, 2005.

Cole, Joanna. *Inside a Beehive*. New York: Scholastic Press, 1996.

Fischer-Nagel, Heiderose and Andreas. *Life of the Honeybee*. Minneapolis: Carolrhoda Books, 1986.

Kalman, Bobbie. *The Life Cycle of a Honeybee*. New York: Crabtree Publishing Company, 2004.

Micucci, Charles. *The Life and Times of the Honeybee*. New York: Ticknor & Fields Books for Young Readers, 1995.

Morris, Ting. *Bee*. North Mankato, MN: Smart Apple Media, 2005.

Sayre, April Pulley. *The Bumblebee Queen*. Watertown, MA: Charlesbridge, 2005.

Schwabacher, Martin. *Bees*. Tarrytown, NY: Marshall Cavendish, 2003.

Spilsbury, Richard and Louise. *A Colony of Bees*. Chicago: Heinemann, 2004.

Films

*Bug City: Bees*. Schlessinger Media, 1998.

*The Life Cycle of the Honeybee*. Reading Rainbow, 1987.

*The Swarm: India's Killer Bees*. National Geographic Television, Inc., 2000.

*Tales from the Hive*. Nova, 2000.

Web Sites

Africanized, Sometimes Called "Killer Bees"
www.insecta-inspecta.com/bees/killer/

Animal Bytes: Bee
www.sandiegozoo.org/animalbytes/
t-bee.html

Apis mellifera: The Common Honeybee
www.earlham.edu/~harrico/
apismellifera.htm

Bee Alert!
grizzly.umt.edu/biology/bees/kid.htm

The Bumblebee Pages
www.bumblebee.org

Honey.com: Just for Kids
www.honey.com/kids/index.html

Nature: Alien Empire
Show 1: Bee Anatomy and Show 2: Enter
 the Hive
  www.pbs.org/wnet/nature/alienempire/
   index.html

   Nova: Tales from the Hive
    www.pbs.org/wgbh/nova/bees/

# Index

Page numbers for illustrations are in **boldface**.

## About the Author

Judith Jango-Cohen's intimate knowledge of nature comes from years of observing and photographing plants and wildlife in forests, deserts, and canyons and along seacoasts. Titles from her forty children's books have been recommended by the National Science Teacher's Association, chosen for the Children's Literature Choice List, and named a Best Children's Book of the Year by the Children's Book Committee at Bank Street College. You can find out more about her books and school visits at www.jango-cohen.com.